Journey
POEMS & SHORT STORIES

by

KEN SKOBY

Illustrations, Photographs and Understanding:
Nancy Tkachuk

Gotham Books

30 N Gould St.
Ste. 20820, Sheridan, WY 82801
https://gothambooksinc.com/

Phone: 1 (307) 464-7800

© 2022 Ken Skoby. All rights reserved.

No part of this book may be reproduced, stored in a retrieval system, or transmitted by any means without the written permission of the author.

Published by Gotham Books (November 17, 2022)

ISBN: 979-8-88775-048-4 (sc)
ISBN: 979-8-88775-049-1 (e)
ISBN: 979-8-88775-050-7 (h)

Because of the dynamic nature of the Internet, any web addresses or links contained in this book may have changed since publication and may no longer be valid.

The views expressed in this work are solely those of the author and do not necessarily reflect the views of the publisher, and the publisher hereby disclaims any responsibility for them.

TIME AND SPEED
ARE INSIGNIFICANT
TO A JOURNEY

HELLO

TABLE OF CONTENTS

POEMS

Suspended 1
Life Interrupts 2
Locked 3
Word 5
Snowfelt 6
Together 7
H2O 10
The Butter Churn 11
Tomorrow 12
The Hourglass 13
Shadows 15
Air 16
Patience 17
The Circle 18
Fear 20
A Giving Soul 21
Shadow Walker 22
Forsaken 23
The Candle 25
Dragonfly 26
Artists 27
Fallen 28

Twelve	29
Serenity	30
The Magicians	31
Life In Illusion	34
The Gifts	35
The Hermit	36
Grey	37
The Storm	38
A Lonely Tree	39
Watchers	41
Twilight Dawn	42
The Grandfather Clock	44
Maples	45
Gardeners	47
Halcyon Morning	48
Tides	49
Snow	50
Quiet Fisherman	51
Silent Mist	53
Caged	55
Hushed	56
Rivers	57
Words	59
The Door	61
This These	62

Assaulted	63
The Search	65
Crystal Bridge	67
Blinded	68
Wounded	69
The Attic	70
Paradise	71
Boiling Pot	73
The Lighthouse	74
Clouds	75
Pieces	76
Conversation	78
The Mountain	79
Seasons	81
Two Fountains	83
The Net	85
Bamboo Heart	86
Dreamer	87
Waterfall	88
Lazy Gaze	89
The Wish	91
Time	92
Thought	93
Reflections	95
Acrobats	96

Letting Go 98

Wolf Moon 99

The Future 100

Stone Mountain 101

Apathy 102

Sponges 104

Whippoorwill 105

RHYTHMIC POETRY

Carry Me 108

Quarantined 109

Puzzled 110

Songs Of The Heart 111

Spring Songs 112

Wine In A Whiskey Glass 113

The Blanket 114

Birth 116

SHORT STORIES

Soul Touch 119

A Friend 120

Dream 123

Lighting Encounters 124

Golden Experience 126

Twin Fawns 128

Knowing Fear 132
The Lost Star 135
Seeds 139
The Odd Ducks 141
The Mola And The Sparrow 144
The Concert 147
Close Encounters 151
The Awakening 158

*Curiosity does not kill,
lack of awareness might*

Snow covered winter trees teach
it is about life within

POEMS

Perceiving she was troubled; I could not depart.
Sitting sullen at the window,
an unmoving silence surrounded the room.
I sat to touch her cup of tears.

Moments were displayed like trophies,
pictures posed strategically upon a shrine.
Unrelenting roses laid draped in a yellow ribbon,
as an unlit scented candle slept, covered in dust.
Plush creatures with silent eyes,
watched as a broken smile held back tears.
Clothed in fragmented thoughts,
a soulful silence robed her eyes.
Only perceiving yesterday,
never seeking tomorrow,
not recognizing this day.

LIFE INTERRUPTS

One soul was freed playing music,
the music e*choes*…
Another was unchained dancing,
the *dance* delays…

Moment's dissolve,
time becomes intense,
freely, seamlessly,
tightly entwining.

Both reach for tenderness,
yet accept passion.
Desperately clasping, softly caressing,
sensing the other's pains.

Hoping for the gentle touch of humanity,
desires float soaring.
Souls release spontaneously.
Silence lingers…

Life interrupts…
               Time became the reaper.

LOCKED

Submerged in yesterday,
distant and apathetic,
somber and unchanging.
Fragments descend,
thoughts languish,
dreams become still.

Wearing memories, sound resonates,
happier reflections weep.
Secluded and languid,
a veneered facade splinters and breaks.
Sheltered in antiquity time suspends,
moments hover and surround.

Interjected moments waver,
benevolence whispers,
thoughts regain visions.
Shadow's slowly wane,
forgotten glimmers erupt,
imagination ignites.

The key reaches…
   Releasing in today.

Yesterday is a place to visit, not live.

WORD

When first discovered,
it lived, breathed and caressed.
Sensing every precious moment,
flooding the heart, mind and body.
Reaching for warmth, it vanished,
tangled and twisted somewhere within life.

Searching for reason, contemplating,
drifting, grasping and connecting.
Somewhere beyond caress,
a gentle serene silence engulfed.
Vibrations flood every sense,
uniting two shared gentle souls.

A whisper, "Do you know how I feel?"
"Yes," was the only answer.
Anxiety rises…
unable to speak the word.
Regret lingers…
a delayed heart burst forth.
      The true essence of the word is exposed;
           a pathway opened.
           Moments are forever.

SNOWFELT

Fresh snow cloaks the woodland,
melodies of color burst forth amid branches.
Gliding winds sail *snow dancers* to freedom,
a glancing sun ignites transcendent crystals.

The sky permeates *drifting* auras,
provoking vibrant flying life to sing.
Curiously prancing from limb to limb,
seeking rhythm from sleeping branches.

A brook's banks, mantled in white,
its cool sapphire veins rush *free*.
Translucent ice grasps for its heart,
its intensity shall not be contained.

Nature resonates, *eyes* reveal shadowed trails,
a forest floor exposes existence.
Perseverance has silently slipped by,
a hushed *smile* follows vanishing tracks.

The air, crisp and pure,
the shroud of snow exposes time's secrets.
Gently, *quietly*, they surge, infinitely.
Unsealed eyes, opened hearts, *realizing* life's *art*.

TOGETHER
Written by: Ken Skoby & Nancy Tkachuk

It rises early creating new frontiers,
glimmers reach beyond the stratosphere.
Its sight ever reaching,
sailing through the atmosphere.
Expelling fire and light,
it reveals its passion.
Its capabilities are fierce and free.

Surrounded by stars, planets and galaxies,
it waxes and wanes as reflections reach.
Its gravitational pull controls oceans flow,
exposing and providing nourishment.
Offering wonder, hope and a sense of rhythm,
its pull regulates wobble at the earth's axis.
It keeps a climate reasonably stable.

It is dynamic, yet formless,
as it moves, it holds the breath of existence.
Levitating clouds and rain,
filtering the sun,
and providing growth to all life.
It delivers highways for flight,
echoes through mountains and breath to winds.

Spinning and balanced in nature,
offering stability, gravity and fertility.
It embraces oceans, rivers, lakes and streams,
mountains, forests, and plants; nourishing insects,
reptiles, mammals, fish, shellfish, fungi and birds.
Its temperamental nature shakes unexpectedly.
Waters may flood without warning,
even the strongest trees may fall.
Envisioning many wonders,
rainbows, sunrises and sunsets,
allowing the ability to imagine and dream.

Together they are vast and ever reaching,
yet none of these gifts are absolute.
They all must live life together,
if one is lost, all are lost.
They all hold time,
yet can be timeless.
They all hold life,
yet work toward extinction.
Only together can they maintain.

The universe could be an endless gift.

Growth is achieved
at imperceptible moments

A magnified droplet exposes a world,
collectively, a universe.
Still or ever flowing,
murky or crystal clear.
Its journey may be in stillness,
or recklessly intense.
Within its cosmos, alien lives flourish.

It cannot be grasped,
nor walked upon,
yet all life flows with it.
Every breath contains it,
yet one cannot breathe within it.
Its molecules reach spaciously
so, one may see beyond.

In the bitter cold stillness,
one may walk upon it,
yet life still flows below.
Life cannot exist without it,
yet it embraces life and death,
its secrets are constantly streaming

H_2O

Cream is poured inside a churn,
light vanishes, its world bound,
life becomes confined.

Within each stroke,
friction creates stress,
waters separate.

Beginning to comply,
the liquid alters,
fluidity gradually suspends.

Feeling the stress,
its flow slows,
flexibility begins.

Salt is added,
molding and shaping,
its transformation complete.

Time flows,
strengthened,
the silhouette softens.

    THE BUTTER CHURN

Suspended…
                        Endlessly floating…
Sheltered beyond time,
always advancing,
yet, never arriving.

Ancient yet new,
persistently perceiving,
a pathway to any thought.

Sensing hopes and dreams,
endless adventures,
for the innocent inventor.

It's a start, not a finish,
a hope and a dream,
it is a sun and a moon.

It is always a beginning,
never a past.
It is a second chance…
                    A wish waiting...

    It is the new day one has not yet lived.

TOMORROW

                    Sitting quietly in silence,
                    humbly listening,
                    as moment's rest.

Never wavering,
understanding,
tolerant to every rotation.
                    Eminent winds blow,
                    rigid rains descend,
                    mountains echo.

Ocean's roar,
a world quivers,
thoughts splinter.
                    Wakening within,
                    its realm revolves,
                    seasons descend.

Softly, silently,
sands gently fall,
slowly slipping away.
                    Flashes of time,
                    drift into memory,
                    concealed, then buried.

Waiting in stillness,
respectfully observing.
Accepting every turn… Understanding.

                    THE HOURGLASS

I would have never found time
If I wore a watch

In a rising or setting sun they are exposed,
they cannot be grasped, yet are attached.

Running towards, one cannot capture,
running from, one shall not escape.

Magically appearing from any direction,
growing far greater than its source.

Many times, they will go unnoticed,
as the sun touches the top of the sky.

They can stretch and reach striking fear,
or shrink slowly, stimulating imagination.

Constantly changing within the light,
appearing as ghosts larger than life.

In clouds of rain or the deepest dark,
they escape like a thief in the night.

SHADOWS

Clouds drift, winds speak,
aromas float and birds soar,
yet it has no burdens.

It shall never resist,
suspending freely,
yet eyes will never see.

Plants grow, rains fall,
snow floats, life scurries,
yet it has no substance.

Its touch is of softness,
its caress encompasses,
yet diluting in its loftiness.

Flourishing in the sky,
seemly unimportant,
yet all life would perish without it.

It has no sight,
it shall never be grasped,
yet we still believe.

AIR

It struggles to resolve,
pursuing reason,
while living the harshness of life.

Discovery quietly rests,
silently expecting,
hopefully waiting in time.

Forever suspending,
possessing no conclusion,
its value clearly understated.

Its wealth, abundant,
the rewards, infinite,
waiting to be unlocked.

When its key is given,
its treasure holds a modest value.
When its key is learned,
forever priceless!

PATIENCE

THE CIRCLE

Below the setting sun,
gypsy winds floated mysterious images.
Long and thinning shadows silently shorten.

Dreams of the night awaken,
senses connect to existence,
stirring the union of life.
Silhouettes of past and future soar,
struggling to find a way,
insignificance silently enters.

Making an escape to true freedom,
ascending within every thought.
Sailing higher and higher,
unusual visions are left behind.
Constellations of sound and color,
brightly shimmer and surround.
Nomadic winds float mysterious images,
thickening shadows grow in the climbing sun,
rising higher it announces a new born day.

In a world of black and white
Gandalf chose grey

Why do you think they called it
Middle Earth?

FEAR

Softly, silently it sneaks,
a moment imperceivable.
                Almost forgotten,
                a passing thought,
                striking again.
Veiled within deceit,
buried in denial,
untruths rise, wisdoms fade.
                Wrapped in a coat,
                feeling warm and safe,
                apathy grows.
Mysteriously life sleeps,
dimly silent,
burrowing deep.
                Manipulations rise,
                spaces thin,
                truths fatally wounded.
Innocence erupts,
flowing lights twinkle,
apathy escapes.
                Birthing glimmers,
                senses clear,
                silence fractures.

A GIVING SOUL

Entering the doors,
pointing a direction,
choosing a corner table.
                A passing glance,
                evading contact,
                hidden, encased in glass.
Wrapped in reflection,
releasing a leather coat,
as if it were the only burden.
                Surrounded in wisdoms,
                yesterdays whispered,
                silence became contagious.
Understanding every passion,
knowing every caress,
yet, always rejecting love.
                Sharing touch,
                with no acceptance,
                always leaving as one.
Rejecting no one,
accepting hypocrisy,
sitting in stillness…

SHADOW WALKER

Unassuming, silently wandering,
shadows waver,
nearing lies explode.
                Deceptions rise,
                restrictions choke,
                life becomes obscure.
Surrounded by hubris,
arrogance and conceit,
lying fatally wounded.
                The walker cries,
                this makes no sense,
                surely there is hope.
Views oppressed,
truths suppressed,
deceit becomes the norm.
                Inside worthless words,
                actions speak,
                spirits perceive.
Shadows disappear,
deprived of light.
Life hesitates within two dimensions.

FORSAKEN

Names become numbers,
words weapons,
freedoms compromised.
                      Voices lay wounded,
                      restrictions choking,
                      truth imprisoned, silent.
Deviously programed,
compassions wane,
resentments begin to swell.
                      Divided and conquered,
                      knowing not concerning,
                      the past rests, withering.
Controlling wealth,
demanding devotion,
liberties lie in shadows.
                      Removing, not giving,
                      interrupting not listening,
                      glaring, not seeing.
Stealing, without earning,
feeling without sensing,
deceits with no remorse.

                      Designs without compassion.

Arrogance only sees itself
humility feels and senses so much more

THE CANDLE

A solitary candle slumbers,
apathetic and languid,
surrounded in darkness.
                Its circular exterior,
                smooth and cold,
                hardened and listless.
Blinded, a hunger grows,
searching within,
existence slowly stirs.
                Enduring isolation,
                knowing apathy and missteps,
                sparks begin to glimmer.
The candle ignites,
its colorful flame dances,
shadows grow in its light.
                It's coat, soft and soothing,
                warmth begins to kindle,
                hope saturates eclipsed air.
In the distance,
faint flames glow,
another, then another.
Flickering silhouettes transform,
now three-dimensional, truths awaken.

DRAGONFLY

A peeking morning sun extends,
sleeping petals yawn.

Existence stirs on a silent pond,
creatures begin to stir.
Crawling from muddy waters,
a water insect clings to a swaying reed.
                Remaining…softly suspended,
                bathing beneath the sun.
                Drying… seemingly hollow,
                its life force expires.
Life has not yet conceded,
it sits in stillness.
Within its dried shell, a birth,
bursting forth in transformation.
                Wilted and bewildered,
                fluttering, drying wings spread.
                Hums float into the air,
                a new life bursts into the blue.
Soaring above jeweled waters,
its kaleidoscopic colors shimmer.
The dying day begins its descent,
blossoms softly rest.

ARTISTS

Their infinite keyboard sails the universe,
endless colors, sounds and scents await.
Imaginations speak as minds reach,
yearnings express a captured dream.

Skillful caresses glide with emotion,
wonders gain sight, obtaining wings.
Sensations soar far beyond,
thoughts freeze moments in time.

Leaving the body, drifting in air,
impressions surround within hues.
Every sense wakens and pulsates,
creativity soars, a released soul speaks.

Tones bleed, reflections achieve sight,
exposing laughter, tears, heartbreaks and wisdoms.
Ambiance surrounds, colors swirl and glow,
a vision freed…

We all walk within rainbows.

FALLEN

A thundering vibration shakes the earth.
Gazing upon the source,
dust concealed its roots,
yet its foundation spoke of life.

Circles stretched outward from its core,
rings chronicle the seasons.
Each space a fragment of time,
persevering beyond every trial.

Weathered, lying silent, skin and arms discarded,
cuts become descriptively alive.
Knots and wounds, bled and hardened,
circles now transformed into lines.

Every grain spoke of endurance,
patience and strength.
Surviving every trial,
a solitary life realized.

The thinnest spaces survived,
so, the widest could flourish.

TWELVE

Morning's golden beams emerge,
blushing colors stretch,
birthing dawn's new day.
                    Hazy minds slowly saunter,
                    peaceful minds race,
                    inundated senses echo.
Thought reflections dwindle,
life's rush activates,
movements become intense.
                    Radiance wanes,
                    lethargic minds dim,
                    crescendos slowly fade.

A silky curtain descends,
exposing a velvet dusk,
color obscures the expiring day.
                    A jeweled sky flourishes,
                    dusks soft veil slowly falls,
                    windows twinkle with light.
Captive souls unwind,
unseen thoughts float,
tranquil senses peacefully repose.
                    Tedious eyes, flicker,
                    minds wander, dreams open,
                    spirits' float.

SERENITY

Deep silence surrounded the darkened forest.
Softly stumbling to a moist moss-covered log,
somewhere between wake and sleep,
beyond the wheels of birth and death,
tranquility quietly conversed.

The first rays of sun extend,
bathing the damp forest floor.
Perceiving light,
seeds open, plants push,
imperceptibly moving earth.

A white mist rose like incense,
hinting of soil and evergreen.
Exhaling nimble winds,
drift tender notes,
souls of the wood awaken.

Shadows morph into color,
trees begin to speak.
Feathered life cheerfully serenades,
wildflower's yawn,
day life surges.

THE MAGICIANS

Choosing a restricted life of illusion,
floating freely no more.
Birth becomes an ever-flowing challenge.

Released from a liquid sheltered womb,
a new breath exhales.
Struggling yet, instinctively feeding,
senses float, thought arrives,
eyes begin to clarify.

Crawling to reach some distant intent,
imagination activates.
Finding a use for awkward legs,
discovering self-movement.

Suspended somewhere in time,
discovering words and tenderness.
Smiles, laughter, tears and happiness,
building foundations that forever remain.

Lessons remain rigid and constant,
as the pains of life slowly drift.
Grasping for tenderness and understanding,
searching to find unconditional love.

Seeking reason, wanderings slow,
investigating thoughts beyond one's own.
Each journey distinctive, every path winding,
as each riddle solved alters perception.

Amazement's surround, minds explore,
mysteries unfold exposing slumbering senses.
Floating beyond, reaching freedom,
spirits soar with the speed of thought.

Escaping time,
magically…
Sailing.

Time is more precious
than possessions or money

LIFE IN ILLUSION

Thoughts drift to a darkened wood,
a full moon glitters the fallen snow,
shades of grey venture.
Gazing through a window,
a new dawn rises,
skies streak in scarlet, saffron and blue.
Perceptively wandering,
deceived eyes,
birth a gentle smile.
Disrupting the rising day,
welcomed life appears,
framed within a deception.
Sounds are hushed,
senses are wildly empty,
lost behind translucent glass.
No roaming winds,
crisp foggy breaths,
or the softness of the snow.
Deprived of life songs,
childish laughter,
the touch of the winds flow.

Silently transformed,
the window had become a wall.

THE GIFTS

Soft spoken with a gentle smile,
knowing eyes held an open heart.
Speaking honestly,
without judgement,
they sensed the other's burdens.

A first touch,
melts into an embrace.
Somewhere beyond passion,
lightning struck; lips caressed,
heartbeats harmonized; two vanish as one.

Relaxed, lying silent,
stillness roared.
Rushing through a lost heart,
innocence awoke.
Transcending memory,
Touched…
   Forever joined.

        Love was not the only gift,
          it was the giving.

            Always

THE HERMIT

Surrounded in silence,
sheathed within walls,
pondering a life.

Reflections awoke,
awareness pulsated,
struggles rest recorded.

Blinded in darkness,
wisdoms stirred,
drifting further within.

Wandering, soaring,
invisible walls shattered,
time became fragile.

Colors illuminated,
soft sensations streamed.
The circle is now complete.

A withered drying frame,
embraces brittle bones,
smiling.

GREY

Caressing breezes emerge,
floating ghosts arise.
The hanging haze saturates the view,
dressing naked trees in a pre-dawn mist.

Gentle pines dressed in green,
sway melodically in a lullaby wind.
Fields, clothed in white,
exposes veiled life's crossing.

Silence engulfs the air,
landscapes begin to shimmer.
Distracting billows glide,
a mind rides hidden winds.

Grey's surrender,
clouds glow pink and red.
A valiant ancient sun peeks,
inserting purple and yellow.

Unmoving portraits linger,
silence speaks…
    Winged day life floats a well-worn path in the sky.

THE STORM

Binding the rising sun,
an obscured mourning sky darkens.
Renegade gusts intensify,
pines are violently persuaded.
Bolts of light shock the sky,
thunder's voice splits the air.

Rigid punishing rains,
strike the landscape,
angry nomadic winds exhale.
The bowing willows weep,
soft pines splinter,
even the mighty oaks shake.

In its darkest hours,
all life shelters,
apprehensions escalate.
Assaulting rains withdraw,
illogical clouds lift,
radical winds gently balance.

                   An imprisoned sun,
          liberates arches of infinite blushes.

A LONELY TREE

Beneath the ageless sky,
a vast swaying meadow awakens.
Traces of flowers and clover wander,
dancing in a quivering field.
In its center, towering above,
an old majestic tree stands tall.
Its heart, well within its massive trunk,
its aged skin splintered and cracked.
Its sheltering branches spread,
dressing its canopy in shades of green.

Above, a dependable sun grins,
below a red-tailed hawk floats.
Escaping feathered life
scatter to sheltering limbs.
A shy rabbit pokes its head about,
returning beneath its roots.
Curious squirrels' glance,
scurrying mice conceal.
Gossiping groundhogs peer about,
pondering the commotion.
With help from a friendly wind,
the tree bows, beaming.

Gazing into the eyes of twin fawns
a long-lost smile
erupted in their reflection

WATCHERS

From the highest peaks to the deepest oceans,
upon earth and deep below; they observe.
Sky spirits inspect the air, earth and trees,
earth spirits walk the surface or burrow deep.
Water spirits swim streams, rivers and lakes,
a few unite with the expansive oceans.

Some equipped with feathered skin and wings,
several covered in shells, fur and even horns.
Others possess scales, fins and tails,
every species multi-colored,
with diverse silhouettes and dimensions.
Quietly they live their lives.

All sense the earth quakes, the waters flood,
and wildfires blindly scorching.
Beneath the sea, plates teeter,
barely holding still.
Predators begin to rise,
the humble, quietly suffer.

Time lingers, all hopefully observe,
the watchers wait.

TWILIGHT DAWN

Stained-glass clouds capture a falling sun,
throwing colors across the sky.
A whispering wind exhales,
day life is peacefully hushed.

Serene silence saturates the air,
as a meditating sky glows.
Surrounded in a momentary truce,
time suspends uninterrupted.

Nocturnal life leisurely awakens,
musical cricket's sing to a purple sky.
Fireflies dance in invisible fields,
emerging distant stars scintillate.

Predators eerily howls, pierce the hollow air,
unseen pulsating wings flutter.
Snapping branches alert the senses,
stealth nightlife is exposed.

Inside the quiet ashen calm,
a rustling wind inhales.
Stained-glass clouds capture a rising sun,
throwing colors to the sky.

Do not bother to chase time,
let it chase you.

THE GRANDFATHER CLOCK

Hundreds of years old, the ancient clock sits,
shuttering, clicking and grinding.
Illuminating paradoxes of the universe,
its ageless bell strikes the hours.
The benevolent pendulum swings back and forth,
pausing imperceptibly, with every swing.

Each passage, secrets of life unfold,
revealing the mysteries of twelve.
Midnight strikes, the clock chimes,
one day dies, as a new one is born.
A new cycle begins.

The antique wood vibrates,
moonlight flickers upon its circular face,
its virtuous creaking voice, lays silent.
Malevolence rises, arrogance meets itself,
ancient wisdoms stir.
The clock winds, the pendulum swings,
time will not falter.

                Tick tock, tick tock,
                  the clock creaks.

MAPLES

Naked maples waver in a callous winter wind.
The last of their clinging withering leaves fall,
its bark protects their suspending hearts.
Feathery lives perch upon their bones.
A low hanging sun warms and softens,
stirring its slumbering stream.

Sweet nectar rushes through their core,
sugar houses throw sweet clouds to the air.
Cascading spring showers birth new life,
jade buds begin to emerge.
Pulsating leaves begin to unfold,
broad veined emerald foliage awakes.

Shaded seeds begin to sprout,
mystical winds glide their flights.
Knowing children throw them skyward,
for a second and third ride.
The extended sun and a harvest moon smile,
chilly autumn winds gust.

Leaves dress in yellow, orange and red,
slowly fading they ride the gusty winds,
seeking the remnants of their journey.

As with the cycle of the maple tree,
many green leaves change color and fall,
as one grows.

GARDENERS

Hoping for a bountiful harvest,
seeds are lovingly planted.
The garden meticulously groomed,
as the sun bathes upon its rich soil.

A couple labors in the spring winds,
planting, feeding, watering and caring.
Roots grow deep, inquisitive plants stretch,
reaching for the warming light.

The two lovingly labor, caring and inspecting,
defending innocence from impetuous weeds.
Caressing and maintaining their labors of love.
The plants begin to sprout and flower.

When fallen, they lifted,
when wounded, they healed,
when weeping, they tended,
managing time for all.

The couple cry, smile, and even argue,
yet the seedlings always came first.
      Without both, together, their harvest
      would never have been so magnificent.

HALCYON MORNING

Spring winds sleep,
a glass lake awaits the rising sun,
circular ripples emerge on its surface.

Kaleidoscopic colors streak the dawn,
birdsongs compose the soundtrack.
Ospreys dive in a silent breach,
as water striders glide.

Muskrats etch the morning glass,
a blue heron stands silent and tall.
Trumpeting geese swim the sky,
duck families proudly cruise.

Water lilies stretch, dragonflies whisper,
dancing breezes softly pirouette.
Wakes swirl in the boggy brush,
tiny waves swoosh the shore.

Rhythm's drift, harmony reaches,
stillness saturates the mind,
imagination soars.

TIDES

Sun-bathed skies descend, softly touching the sea.
Curious winds caress the curling surf,
exposing the breathing shore.

Barefoot children splash into a frigid sea,
screams float the air,
retreating into the warming sands.

Tides withdraw dropping treasures,
waters slowly rise.
Stories of footprints quietly wash away.

Every day reveals a circle,
as serene sounds touch the senses.
Birthing the silent mind.

*When one cannot find time,
change life!*

SNOW

Reminiscent of milkweed,
floating the late summer blue,
soft fluffy snowflakes waltz inside the air.

A gentle downy blanket slowly rises,
darkness descends, as life sounds soften.
Drifting the hours of darkness,
silence sails, lights glow a foggy saffron.

A rising sun ignites a wonderland,
gusty boasting winds swirl and blow.
Glittering colors reflect in the sky,
excited children patiently wait.

A first jump from the stairs,
chilly faces wear red, breath gains sight.
Giggling in wonder, imagination's soar,
spheres take shape, a first snowball thrown.

Pure joy suspends within the air,
diving in snow banks, making snow angels.
All under the watchful eyes of a grinning snowman.

QUIET FISHERMAN

Sounds of a scurrying stream fill the air,
falling waters cascade over unmoving rocks.
A light mist throws colors into serene eyes,
stillness awakens with a peering morning sun.

A shadowed bank unveils movement,
young minks play among the rocks.
Scents of earth, water and wildflowers
glide across a soft dreaming breeze.

Avian life begins to surround the scenery,
skimming still waters for a morning meal.
Fish rise, ducks land and preen,
discarded leaves and branches float slowly by.

High above great birds float the blue,
billowy clouds capture the mind.
Time softly floats, smiles erupt,
casting the line, pondering,
watching ripples disappear.

The fisherman pauses below the sinking sun.

My parents use to say:
"Use your head for something
other than a hat rack."
So, I never wore a hat...
Except while fishing!

When the early bird catches the worm,
it does not mean it will catch a fish.

SILENT MIST

Dark rolling clouds bind the light,
torrential rains pierce the calm.
Heavy tempos beat forests and fields,
oppressive torrents rigidly descend.
Disrupted lakes and streams rise,
violent droplets ignite surface halos.

Unseen thirsty roots pulsate,
yet they cannot drink.
Distressed waters intensify,
submerged banks erode.
Cadences rapidly escalate,
vibrant scents slumber.

Burdened flowers bow,
rigid plants snap and fall.
Crescendos slowly soften,
droplets slip from burdened life.
Dry captive roots absorb,
swirling clouds dissipate,
light races across the sky.

A soft silent mist suspends,
exposing breathing ghostly light.

Tenderly, a pale rainbow reflects,
dew brightly glitters,
sheltered life begins to stir.
Quietly a comforting breeze exhales,
aromas ride a whispering air,
forest beings scurry into the shortened day.

A storms intensity cannot be sustained,
renegade phantom winds depart.
Life sounds gently drift the air,
balance resonates and restores.
Silhouettes will always seem larger,
just before darkness falls.

Life waves as the candle flame,
dusk and dawn unite.
A silent mist strengthens.

CAGED

Captive bodies pace, starving eyes search,
inadvertently detained behind glass.

Time seemingly stagnates,
reflective minds contemplate release.

Thoughts blindly wander, confusions escalate,
strength begins to dwindle.

Life becomes unbending, voices are confined,
points of view splinter.

Time remains constant, truth never wavers,
deceptions are revealed.

Souls illuminate, senses sharpen,
wisdoms expand and grow.

Self-inflicted wounds heal,
perseverance set them free.

    Soul's escape.

HUSHED

Serenity saturates the living air,
sunset pauses on a painted horizon.
Closing bird songs quietly suspend,
trees softly float a sizzle cymbal.

Fragrances travel on a humming wind,
twilight reveals familiar silhouettes.
Colorful curtains radiate and fade,
silence overwhelms the eyes.

Nature grasps a momentary peace,
insects begin to speak, fireflies ignite.
A withering breeze drops a satin cloak,
captured lights begin to glimmer.

Deep darkness perches,
illuminations clothe the sky.
Star's flicker, green, blue and bright,
a full moon yawns.

RIVERS

Flows wander, currents vary,
wildly raging when shallow,
still and calm when deep.
Each path endlessly fluctuating,
every obstruction humbly deflects,
yet its visions do not concede.

Repelling unmoving obstacles,
nimbly adapting and flowing.
Unaware in time,
journeying ever forward.
Not expecting or waiting,
flowing to reach its destined intent.

Accepting floods and drought,
balancing life and death,
rejecting no arrivals.
Emotionally streaming,
constantly progressing,
reaching to share with the sky and sea.

Paths may alter,
journeys are ever flowing.

WORDS

Harbingers of love, life and lessons,
releasing the freedom of laughter,
the tears of loss and the torture of fear.

Softly they reflect thoughts,
sincerely, they speak of visions,
manipulated, blankets of illusion.

Yielding as a summer breeze,
lifting as an epiphany,
or rigid as the stone.

Holding smiles of wisdom,
evolutions of thought,
pains from deceit.

Revealing the beauty of love,
implications of feelings,
or the shattering of an innocent's wind.

Delivering dreams of hope,
the gentleness of whispers,
yet, they are only words.

Too many flowery words,
leave a distinct aroma.

Truth enters into the heart and mind,
Harsh words enter into the ears...
There is no need for them to go further.

THE DOOR

Behind a door the unknow sleeps,
imaginary whispers begin to speak,
hesitation ponders, uncertainty lingers.

A mind races, a heart pulsates,
confidence wanes, fantasy fears rise.

Mysterious images escalate,
interrupted life awaits on the other side.

Resolution enters, a hand extends,
the knob turns, a door swings open.

Awestricken, senses surge,
eyes reflect, marvels smile.

New endeavors no longer wait,
realizing, doors open from both sides.

*First reflections
may not contain final images.*

THIS THESE

These hands have touched,
softness and rigidity,
unpleasantness and beauty,
while grasping traces of life.

This heart has sensed,
agony and ecstasy,
apathy and devotion,
while pondering the wonder of smiles.

These eyes have seen,
hate and compassion,
new life and mortality,
and visions one cannot explain.

This mind has reached,
learning and understanding,
assisting and sensing,
hoping existence becomes one.

These feet have voyaged,
with every this and these,
yet, I am just a child in the universe.

ASSAULTED

Gradually deception creeps,
words fall distorted.
Lies shot so swiftly,
pierce as bullets from a gun.

Puppets attack with fear,
emblazoned greed saturates.
Profound innocents sacrificed,
wolves are at the door.

Technologies censor,
freedoms are locked.
Peoples divide,
vultures own the air.

Ruthlessly, meticulously,
a tangled web is weaved.
Venomous spider's quickly strike,
their webs capture every thought.

Curtains become doors,
doors become bars,
bars imprison.

Riches and poverty
are words of many lessons

THE SEARCH

Walking the unconscious streets,
the night sky cannot be reached.
Flaring lights and sounds inundate,
dazed, a seeker slowly wanders.

Unoccupied people scurry,
grasping flashing rectangles.
Walking aimlessly blind,
oblivious to benevolence.

Stunned emotionless robots,
steer empty hollow shells.
Speaking into stagnate air,
recklessly distracted.

Inside pulsating windows,
sleepwalkers sit.
Gazing mesmerized,
into large flickering boxes.

Drifting beyond the artificial day,
gazing upon grass and bushes.
Vague stars dimly speckle the sky,
house windows flash hypnotizing light.

Inside were young children,
embracing gleaming tablets.
Dazed overcome parents stare,
no laughter drifted the yard.

Bewildered, the wanderer continues,
searching for traces of inspiration.
A glowing peaceful dwelling appears,
the seeker slows, smiles and remains.

Nature began to speak,
as all of existence instructed.
Trust filled the fields, forests and skies,
rekindled wisdoms quickly grew.

Night blazed into a brilliant star filled sky,
drifting softly in a reflective moons light.
Pausing in fields, contemplating with fireflies,
mind speak began to blossom.

Together sharing secrets of the cosmos,
listening to the keyboard of the universe.
Witnessing together birth and death,
grasping all the ambience of life.
Wondering…

CRYSTAL BRIDGE

Seeking a threshold,
climbing ever higher,
an abysses edge,
slows a passage.

Realizing marvels, tranquility woke,
a crystal bridge sparkled.
Suspending above its center,
gazing into the face of eternity.

Far below, a great river flowed.
Appearing as a silver thread,
it swayed in the wind,
nimbly sailing free.

Within the speed of thought,
drifting past the clouds and blue,
lights glittered brightly,
accenting a soft purple sky.

Stars, planets and galaxies,
gleamed of blue, green and red.
Silence resonated,
the universe swirled with life.

BLINDED

A sun turns black,
a moon glows red,
skies shadow,
curtains close.

Life distressed,
the hollow crumble,
oceans swell,
rivers gasp.

Mountain's moan,
a planet wobbles,
bright stars veil,
galaxies ponder.

The rock crumbles,
streams thirst.
breath captured,
growth withers.

Eye's stumble,
mind's release,
blinded.
Sensing darkness.

WOUNDED

Unseen and silent it cuts,
burrowing deep inside.
Lost, wandering blindly,
descending eyes cloud.

Sorrows and pains conceal,
hidden lesions slowly dwindle.
Veiled compassions are glimpsed,
yet seemingly, so far away.

Discovering so many share wounds,
foggy eyes begin to clear and ascend.
Hope begins to flicker as the flame,
forgotten feelings emerge and elevate.

Moments of life twist and turn,
one cannot love without heartaches.
Heal the broken wing, soar once again,
wisdoms will awake within every step.

> Scars of the body and heart mend,
> unhealed scars of the mind
> wound endlessly.

THE ATTIC

Veiled and dusty, almost forgotten,
precious memories rest.
Shared with absent souls,
cherished thoughts flash in time.

Smiles in a box, tears on a card,
photographs sustain treasured details.
Flickering minds caress the moments,
captured lives carry fond reflections.

Tenderly they beckon the heart,
time floats back into the days.
Summoning priceless words,
teachings that inspired deep within.

Reminiscing the innocent seasons,
before the harshness of life.
Wearing cherished knowledge,
realizing memories are never ending.

> They could not take their wealth with them,
> so, embrace it all, until you see them again.

PARADISE

Sitting on the edge of a breathing meadow,
a small quaint cabin enhances the view.
A warm glow cruises through the sky,
as mighty trees stand tall and free.

Gently swaying to a beckoning wind,
dancing shades of flowers mesmerize.
Colorful scents hang on a resting horizon,
landscapes reflect in a peaceful glow.

Enchanted wings soar a comforting air,
avian songs suspend in the crimson sun.
Hummingbird's rush to their evening meal,
mourning doves emotionally croon.

A dreamy silence softly whispers,
ghostly deer magically appear,
fawns run and playfully bounce.

Bidding farewell to a waning day,
tiny lights flicker within the fields.

        In a world filled with wonder,
        nothing compares to inner beauty.

Tranquility is a gift,
reflect as it blossoms.

BOILING POT

Resting upon a silent stove,
a pot of clear innocent water sits.
Calm, still and free,
undisturbed as it reflects.

A rigid intense glow ignites,
molecules begin to separate.
Quietly a light mist arises,
impatience covers the pot.

Stirring water begins to speak,
rising droplets cling to the lid.
Steam rages, air bubbles rise,
wildly overflowing seeking freedom.

The constraining lid releases.
countless droplets evaporate,
rising into the atmosphere.
The angry fading glow expires.

The reduced waters calm,
reflecting a peaceful silence.

THE LIGHTHOUSE

High above a rocky precipice,
its circular exterior towers.
Piercing the deepest darkness,
warning of danger with its brilliant light.

Strong and steady the beacon searches,
carving through an ever-changing sky.
Inside its cool muffled walls,
a spiraling staircase coils upward.
Suggestive of discarded snail shells
deposited to a damp speaking sand.

Levitating on the endless horizon,
a benevolent sun gently floats.
Misty shadows begin to fade,
breathing waves split the skyline.

Far below a rising sea slaps the rocks,
seaweed sways within its rhythm.
Sounds of hungry gull's saturate the air,
terns glide the unpredictable surface.
Breezes carry the scent of salty air,
foam floats the edges of the living sea.

CLOUDS

High in the stratosphere suspending,
thinly stretching and reaching.
Icy cold, sheer and delicate,
sailing slowly in the sparse air.

Just below, darkened layered patches soar,
donning curling wings of white and grey.
Everchanging wispy edges extend,
slowly feathering across the blue.

Lower still, billowy, fluffy, clouds,
throw auras through the atmosphere.
Glimmers of vividly painted visions,
activate every imagined fantasy.

Visualized thoughts quietly soar,
everchanging cotton billows suspend.
Colorfully hovering across the sky,
sharing with the perishing day.

A reflective sun falls,
igniting the clouds concealed hues.

PIECES

Floating within childlike wonder,
every contact exposes a new sense.
Marks and lesions alert perception,
fragments of innocence slip away.

Excited minds caress emotion,
intense sensations gust in the wind.
Detours in life awaken confusions,
wounded passions just slip away.

Minds wander seeking connection,
ghosts hover, but cannot be grasped.
Virtue surrounded, standing alone,
benevolence quietly slips away.

Escaping turmoil, exploring forests,
Nature's marvels gently reach and stir.
Pure joy of absolute trust blossoms,
innocence burst forth; whispers shout.

Floating within a universe's wonder,
interaction reignites neglected sight.

Dreams are visions of one's reach

CONVERSATION

Unread letters slumber upon a page,
cold and lifeless in search of meaning.
No trace of breath or hints of nuance,
lacking emotion awaiting a vibrant song.

No depth of thought or inspiring wonder,
no exchanges of unique interpretations.
Unspoken words race to the eyes and mind,
vibrations still hang in a wandering hush.

A voice shouts, another whispers,
the silent listen to comprehend.
As words are shared a trust grows,
connections deliver tolerance.

Words express every journey,
all carry a truth to speak.
Anger delivers silence,
Smiles, the gift of friendships.

THE MOUNTAIN

Gazing high above, clouds shroud,
its peak seems insurmountable.
Stepping into the wood line,
a destination can no longer be seen.

All steps lead forward and upward,
awakening the perceptions of life.
Winds carry whispers of stirring water,
igniting a quest to serene echoes.

High above the smiling rocks,
a stream falls into a still pool.
Mists float casting hues below,
trout suspend in their atmosphere.

Quiet paces of an arriving native slows,
nodding at the invader of its domain.
Silently they converse and slip away,
each continuing their separate journeys.

Stepping from the forest gusty winds sail,
reverberation's hush, the remote air thins.
A light snow-covered summit towers,
deep ravines cut through its face.

Walking into the heart of a cloud,
a cool damp energy intensifies insight.
Its yielding veil drifts, time becomes still,
hands reach up into a philosophical sky.

Far below, the peaceful valleys are hushed,
yet the unforgiving slope comes alive.
Birds flutter within the low brush,
a butterfly lands among the blooms.

Every marvel interrupts a wandering mind,
as senses transform, time makes its escape.
Pondering now; what lies far below?
Every step is new, every thought changed.

Forward movement never fails

SEASONS

The time of rebirth rises with the faithful sun.

Impatient winds gust, billows surge across the sky.
The bare and brown bloom into buds of green.
Varied rains nourish, dew coats the morning grass.
Fog floats down the valleys, its spirit is released.
Birth explodes, life flourishes, fragrances dance.
The dormant stir, choruses of time glide in song.

A devoted sun stretches, benevolent light extends,
cooling winds whisper, countless life sounds talk.
Rivers and streams slow, lakes reflect tranquilly,
clouds suspend, the moon and stars intensify.
Across fields lights flicker, night sonatas escalate,
silent curtains fall; night beings stir in shadows.

The sun's rays shorten, light begins its descent,
the harvest moon reflects, illuminating darkness.
Air cools, colors explode, leaves begin their wane,
lightning bolts sever the sky; thunder speaks.
Mists rest in damp hollows, warnings of a freeze,
hail strikes, winds bite, vibrance slowly withers.

A low hanging sun floats the chilly morning sky,
icy fingers extend, frost paints the morning glass.
Symmetrical crystals linger, then slowly vanish,
wintery gusts circle, snowflakes silently descend.
Slowly weaving a blanket, sheltering life below,
seasons become mirrors; reflections sealed in time.

Earth's secrets yield

TWO FOUNTAINS

Two fountains flow…

One with two colorful eyes to gaze, smile or tear,
arms and hands that caress, feel and even grasp.
A mouth that breathes, taste and converses,
a nose that inhales fierce or tender aromas.
Capturing confined reverberations and echoes,
two ears translate, compile and transmit.
A skillful mind decodes all senses,
collecting and storing complex thoughts.
Somewhere in time, it shall touch death.

The second fountain cascades up seeking release,
soaring infinitely through an open universe.
It is seldom seen, and cannot be grasped,
yet it converses while walking in dreams.
It knows no obstruction drifting freely,
every sense, infinitely enhanced.
Perceiving all vibrations, flowing endlessly,
this fountain is far beyond flesh and blood,
it shall never touch death.

Yet, the two are one.

Birth and death are both
an end and a beginning

THE NET

Generations in the making,
meticulously woven square by square,
each weave smaller in time.
Thrown high into the air,
it drifts and descends,
into the deepest depths.
Slowly dragging from above,
all in its path are captured,
for every species there is no escape.

Struggling to reach a distant freedom,
the small and fearless shelter near rock.
The winch tightens and slowly rises,
bound and contained the innocent fall.
Day after day, again and again,
multitudes are trapped and restricted.
Caught in a net of their own making,
tribulations wonder.

What happened?

BAMBOO HEART

A tropical sun gazes into a jungle's depths,
sheltered below its vast foliage, existence stirs.
Moist soil bursts, an exotic sprout explodes,
extending at a rate nearly incomprehensible.

Every day's growth speeds feet into the air,
leaving its mark as a circular ring.
Its core, seemingly hollow,
yet its strength is clearly unrivaled.
In its infancy providing nourishment,
in its youth providing clothing,
as an adult proving shelter and clean air.

Its smooth cool exterior hardens,
yet persistently bows to deceiving winds.
Always giving more than it has taken,
forever smiling in the crying skies.
Carrying no burdens, stretching for the sun,
waiting to be understood.

Clearly there must be more,
to a bamboo heart.

DREAMER

Head in the clouds, coasting softly,
searching for remnants of what was.
Discovering splendors at every turn,
smiles release, gliding within the sky.

Boundless amazements expose,
thoughts rush through the mind.
Every organism quietly connecting,
all life touching earth, unite as one.

A peaceful hush envelopes,
independence drifts in a lingering wind.
Creations begin to quiver,
quiet secrets are kept in waiting.

Restrictions extend beyond extreme,
wounded words wither, humanity splinters.
Conversations are covered in dust.
Harmony sleeps in the ruins.
Freedom weeps.

            A dreamer reawakens.

WATERFALL

In the distance a deafening roar floods the air,
a winding river's hurried flow, silenced.
Thunderous wails hypnotically captivate,
waters reach an edge and exploded below.

Below vibrant voiceless colors float a silent mist,
hushed life scurries, yet there is no echo.
Quavers wander, beating as a drum,
bellows of descending waters surround.

Lost in a freefall within misty hues,
its captured soul releases and unites.
Ageless in its wander, backwash lingers,
memory slows a tempo, serenity restores.

Past the river's rage, whispers are overdue,
pounding blows soften; reflections reappear.
Soft notes reemerge, senses ride a breeze,
a sun's warm rays shine upon a distant waterfall.

Hidden in its energy,
cascades the aromas of life.

LAZY GAZE

A welcoming sun smiles,
great puffy clouds dot the deep blue sky.
Friendly chickadees land in an oak above,
lazy day, lazy day, lazy day, they sing.

A caterpillar slowly takes a stroll up a milkweed,
searching for the perfect leaf for its transformation.
Murmuring winds wave over the fields of hay,
grasshoppers' flit in and out, colorful birds swoop.

Tall grasses and daisies bend against the breeze,
as small life scurries below, going about their day.
Regal birds float, surveying the breathing field,
ever-changing marshmallow clouds leisurely float.

A colorful field spider meticulously weaves a web,
a virtual marvel of engineering, finely crafted.
Strategically capturing the last of the setting sun,
and the colorful glittering of the morning dew.

As a wonder filled mind wanders,
it captures every priceless moment.
The fading day passes much too quickly!

Through the eyes of
True or False,
Right or Wrong
There is no Middle Ground.

THE WISH

Abused and confused an innocent mind wanders,
soft and silent, wandering in search of answers.
Quiet burdens of invisible scars follow every step,
confused tears fall surrounding moments alone.

Unplanned thoughts race, searching blindly,
as descending eyes sorrowfully stroll.
Time escapes, nights are everlasting,
tomorrows never seem to arrive.

Senses numb, imprisoned, seeking escape,
suspicious of every spoken word.
Lost in emptiness, struggling,
roaming aimlessly, searching for a connection.

Quietly sauntering by,
a stranger slows and speaks.
"I sense your pain; it is not your fault."
"I wish for you the light of hope."

Thunderstruck, a single joyful tear
slips down from brightening eyes.
A courageous smile is born.

TIME

In these moments we share,
time remains constant.
Day yields to night,
night yields to day.

We are born, wondering, absorbing,
growing, maturing and aging.
Yet, some are lost so early,
as others paths seem so long.

We reach to touch a hidden goal,
chasing life as the overwound clock.
We float in air and ride the breeze,
yielding and enduring every tempest.

Happiness seems to race,
sorrows seem to lock.
What do we want?
What do we truly need?

Release all burdens,
embrace contentment,
live this day.
Leave death to time.

THOUGHT

What triggers thought?

It can be a sound or scent,
a taste or touch, even an image before us.
Transporting peace or sorrow,
deception or truth, possibly even anxiety.
It may deliver a smile or tear,
float serenity or run turbulently wild.

Thoughts can be escapes or dungeons,
fantasies or fictions, even comedies or drama.
Thought ignites pure imagination,
nothing more, until written or tested.
Thought must be studied, spoken or discarded,
it alone is dangerously one sided.

Are thoughts a harbinger of fear?
Thought may lead us to many mirrors,
yet thought is where we guide it to be.
We are capable of avoiding and blocking thought!
Find the quite place in your mind
where there is no thought.

Honor yourself!

Thought is a guide
Words are a reflection

REFLECTIONS

I don't know who I was,
but I know who I am,
and I know what I can be.

I have lived passionately,
experienced so much,
yet shall never absorb it all.

I have less than what I had,
more than what I need,
with no need for excess.

I hold an innocent's tear,
heartaches and pains,
while embracing the magic of laughter.

I have shared birth and death,
symphonies floating through air,
wonder filled constellations of life and light.

I don't know who you are,
but, for what it's worth,
I wish the same for you.

ACROBATS

Life is similar to the tightrope.

We may advance forward or backward,
yet if we stand still, we shall surely plummet.
We may grasp for wealth and possessions,
yet the more we acquire, the heavier the load.

Because the tightrope is a narrow path,
we do not dwell on hovering or shaky steps.
Eyes gaze forward, seldom looking back,
within every step we are learning balance.

When we achieve; we smile.
When we learn; we assist.
When we receive; we share.
When we fall; we all reach.

When words become hollow;
we should strive for perception.
We always strive to understand.

Written words hold more reflection than spoken.
However, the two together are invincible.

The only colors that matter
are the lights that we reflect

LETTING GO

Submersed in the deep waters of silence,
the tranquil mind surrenders.
Humility and insignificance stretch,
a ghostly mist soars freely.

Void of thought, consciousness enters,
glimpses of universes emerge.
Lost wisdoms hover,
the unlocked mind receives.

Releasing all to sense more,
auric pulses shine brightly.
Drifting within freedom,
whispers become intense.

A keyboard stretches,
color and sound unite,
each note a subtle hue.
infinitesimal creatures expand.

Wonders glide and slow,
once again restricted,
returning to a life of illusion.

WOLF MOON

The full moon's cold winter glow
gently floods a bedroom window.
Its soft hushed light bathes the room,
a quiet soul rests in reflection.

The grey hushed snow relaxes,
a blue moon's intensity stretches.
Awaiting a mysterious sign,
profound silence suspends,

Remnants of lessons drift freely,
smiling tears fall upon a pillow.
Moments in fragments appear,
past journeys race across time.

In the distance a dog howls,
echoes resonate the silent mind.
Closed eyes reach for perception,
as a soul escapes to freedom.

Sparkling eyes quietly open,
a deep quiet breath exhales.

THE FUTURE

STONE MOUNTAIN

Miles above the thinning air,
a snowcapped mountain peak towers.
Withstanding earthquakes, volcanoes
twisted winds and violent storms.

Great living boulders shake and crack,
landslides fall silently, deep below.
Deep within its ancient walls
suspends a heart of stone.

Generations of gentle rains crack its facade,
venting its open heart to the world.
Imperceptibly it slowly beats,
miniscule signs of life live within.

Light bathes the inner sanctum,
liberating a feathery light.
Sound and colors stimulate,
an exposed heartbeat pulsates,
its melodic rhythm soothes.

Newly discovered panoramas smile.

APATHY

Childish laughter from the wood,
communicating beyond understanding,
as all surroundings become one.

Standing naked in the world
soul notes sing.
Unheeded, they just slipped away.

Soft caresses of tenderness,
held loosely in a heart,
slowly escaping in a storm.

Seeking here and there,
loneliness overflowed.
Still, it seemed to be everywhere.

Voices softly spoke,
stirring the lost and dormant.
It slowly makes its escape.

Perceptions begin to rise,
fears drift and fade.
All hopefully standing as one.

Wisdom
When words and actions are one

SPONGES

Submerged in water quietly waiting,
groping and encompassing life.
Breathing and filtering
the nutrients that surround.

Multi-colors and proportions,
hold smooth flexible exteriors.
So carefully harvested,
arriving into a new dimension.

Bathed and drying,
exhaling a first new breath.
Existence changes,
spellbound in a new domain.

Every thought, sound and touch,
becomes captured memories.
Inhaling, exhaling,
softly reaching and observing.

Absorbing all that surrounds.

WHIPPOORWILL

Dusk releases its first veil,
in the edges of the wood,
wings flutter and roost,
a night bird nestles.

Feathers of brown and black,
with a collar accented in white.
Above its massive beak,
thin hairs protrude.

As the second shaded veil descends,
the bird sits quietly alone.
How strange and unusual it looks,
then it speaks its name, again and again.

Soothing sounds of serenity,
flow from its mouth.
Its beauty now revealed,
a song from beyond the universe.

> In the stillness of night,
> there is beauty inside.
> Say your name, sing your song.

Our most valuable gift
is what we hold inside us
Share Sing

RHYTHMIC POETRY

CARRY ME

When I am not aware,
with a blank empty stare.
Lend me your wisdom… Talk with me.

If I cannot receive,
and do not perceive.
Lend me your senses…Reach for me.

When I cannot touch,
sensing is too much.
Lend me your heart…Feel for me.

If I crash land,
and can no longer stand.
Lend me a shoulder...Walk with me.

When I am too weak,
and cannot speak.
Lend me your words…Comfort me.

If I cannot be there,
do not despair,
lend me a memory…I will carry you.

QUARANTINED

Renegade winds test soft-hearted pines,
as birches yield, awaiting the signs.
Humbling trials assist one to grow,
as falling rains feed a forest's glow.

Time ambles forward, each passing day,
thoughts are extended, molding like clay.
Clouds float swiftly when concealing sun,
hours vanish when all's said and done.

Hummingbird's flicker, as air vibrates,
soaring in stillness shatters souls' gates.
Departing windows, floating the blue,
dimensions waver, strangely subdued.

Minds seek freedom escaping the hate,
rejecting bonds, releasing their weight.
Soaring space to other dimensions,
shedding bonds of earthly connections.

New lights rising in amber and gold,
breathing in water, new life unfolds.
Beyond shadows past the atmosphere,
floating, traversing the stratosphere…*Released*.

PUZZLED

Fragments reclining seeking a sun,
shapes and colors, relaxing as one.
Silhouettes searching flickering lights,
linking bonds of equivalent flights.

Concealed inside, each distinctive piece,
mystic edges, will not seek release.
Irrelevant bits, slip through the hand,
yet every piece is part of the plan.

Sensations appear, feelings seek sight,
waking to answers, outlines unite.
Edges forming, define the borders,
shades uniting, filling the corners.

Profile's form and begin to adhere,
messages gather, stories appear.
Complexity is becoming clear,
figures fused, linking a new frontier.

Memories grow,
   when feeling split,
      grasping for locks,
         when the pieces fit.

SONGS OF THE HEART

Loving so deeply, not letting go,
songs so melodic, drifting their glow.
Living so fast, not viewing the cost,
floating the wind, entombing the lost.

Sun bowing freely birthing the night,
shadows growing before taking flight.
Darkness rises, before one can see,
senses awaken, setting one free.

Speaking of truth with nothing to say,
grasping at love, as it slips away.
Pursuing light to revive the soul,
revealing life has taken its toll.

We all hear music, songs of the heart,
wisdom appears before we depart.
Smile with life at every dawn,
trails of the heart are never gone.

SPRING SONGS

A brusque breeze, eases the freeze,
    birds begin to sing.
Wisps drifting by, across the sky,
    surely signs of spring.

Souls drift along, sensing a song
    in the atmosphere.
Walking in mud, trees are in bud,
    crocuses are here!

Notes float above, songs of a dove,
    sing a memory.
Softening leaves, of last year's trees,
    gently resting free.

Scurrying squirrels, looking for pearls,
    always on the run.
The songs are clear, they just appear,
    all becoming one.

Whites shifting green, painting a scene,
    nothing can compare.
All notes arrive, verses come alive,
    music rides the air.

WINE IN A WHISKEY GLASS

Gazing beyond the midnight sun,
searching for reason, finding none.
Seeking a light, gazing for home,
time ticking like a metronome.
Mind's distortions, lives drift apart,
just another hole in the heart.

Wasted time feeling jealousy,
feeling wounded, no one could see.
Lacking wisdom, gold turns to brass,
drinking wine from a whiskey glass.

Memories soar when the winds blow,
lives awaken as the mind grows.
Paths may alter throughout the years,
insights arrive, shedding some tears.
Inner strength is inside us all,
pride shall release after a fall.

Reflections teach, neither was right,
unbound egos, regain true sight.
Lacking lyrics, gold turns to brass,
drinking wine from a whiskey glass.

THE BLANKET

Soft and warm, releasing the storm,
dreams begin to wander.
Safe and sound, all worries are bound,
life is surely changing.

Ignoring facts, reposed and relaxed,
existence releasing.
Ponder, debate, as thoughts meditate,
lives denied of time.

Moment's escape, when shielded and draped,
concealed within deception.
Constantly alone, life in a phone,
deceitfully veiled, sightless.

The rattlesnake's kiss
is hard to miss,
lying comfortably numb.
The hollow within,
it's sink or swim,
when cleverly disguised.

There is something inside! The blanket is alive!
When did this blanket fill with fear?

Fear is our greatest enemy

BIRTH

Closed eyes and ancient minds,
appear inside a womb.
A whisper from the sky soars,
soft wings land within a bloom.

Movement faintly resonates,
as a life begins to form.
Wonders begin to kindle,
as lightning in a storm.

Reaching for an escape,
a marvel now unbound.
Released to an illusion,
vocal freedom is found.

Time holds the reasons,
why we are earthly bound.
Release will only happen,
when answers are found.

We all arrive from uniting,
connecting with eternity.

A journey past happiness
leaves more than one behind

Our choices are infinite
decisions arrive as one

SHORT

STORIES

SOUL TOUCH

A portrait-perfect day in late spring reflected upon the deck overlooking the backyard. Gazing past the fruit trees and gardens, peering into the woods below, lyrical winds supported aromas of lilacs and alyssum. Distracted, darting eyes swept to the descended vines that cascaded from the upper garden to the stones below. Several hummingbirds fluttered in and out of the trumpeted flowers, who's colors had exploded into bloom, apparently overnight. The birds hovered into a break dance, as the air became saturated in a methodical beat. Seemingly from nowhere, a single hummingbird flew directly to my face, a foot away, lingering, staring into surprised eyes. Mesmerized, feeling soft rushes of air and the humming vibrations of wings, we gazed into each other's souls. Sounds were still, hearts pulsated, as a quiet smile stretched gaping lips. In those unexpected precious moments, two souls connected, reaching within.

Flying over to the trumpet vines it joined in the dance with friends

A FRIEND

I had spent many happy moments fishing the small meandering waters of the Alewife Brook, in the town of Essex, Massachusetts. In early spring, alewives would run through the brook so thick you could catch them in your hands. Not many believed my adventures of catching and releasing hundreds of these fish. So, daily, I would challenge anyone to come and try it with me. Finally, someone agreed, so we made plans for the following day. Sharing the same passion, fishing, we both eagerly awaited the following day.

It was the perfect day as we met up at the brook smiling. He was a quiet tranquil young man, tall and lanky, with a thoughtful, almost animated gait. His shoulder length hair was always bound in a red bandana that accented his circular wire rimmed glasses that were suspended on the tip of his nose. He was always seemingly deep in thought.

We walked and shared life as we reached our destination. We ventured into the cool water, meandering around pools, until we reached the perfect spot. It was a stretch of ankle-deep water between two deeper pools. Wildflowers decorated the banks gliding calming aromas through the air. The sun shone through the canopy of trees, leaving dancing gems upon the moving waters. We could see fish everywhere, the fish surrounded us instantly. Gazing over to this normally laid-back person, a neglected smile erupted from his face. His eyes were filled with the joy of a child, as he splashed wildly here and there. Dancing as if fireworks were exploding around him, the fish eluded him. It was then I shared the secret of catching alewives. "Stand still, put your hands in the water, wait for them to come to you, then grab." In no time, he was catching one right after the other.

Sounds of laughter and splashing fish escaping our hands, filled the air, as the fish continued their journey upstream. We were having so much fun, hours seemed to pass in minutes. We finally realized the time, so we ventured back to the road and headed for work.

We walked briskly to the center of town still laughing and smiling, pondering the day that would not be forgotten. With our destination in sight, my friend suddenly stopped, as a devious smile erupted from his face. Walking back toward a police car that we had just passed, he stopped and picked up a plastic six-pack ring with something stuck inside of it. I held my breath, thinking, what is he up to? Walking directly up to the police car he knocked on the window. As the chief of police rolled down the window, my new friend lifted up the six-pack ring, which now, I could tell had a dead alewife stuck through it. Smiling and shaking his head from side to side he declared, "There you go chief, another alcohol related death."

    Grinning, we slowly sauntered to work
ready to share our stories.

Memories are tears and smiles
that keep giving

DREAM

I once journeyed to a faraway place and witnessed everyone working in harmony, smiles and laughter filled the air. As I gazed about, a stranger asked if I needed any guidance. "I was wondering where one might go to take in this beautiful day." Without a word, pointing in the direction of a grassy knoll. "Thank you, sir," I said, venturing to the perfect spot to relax and let my thoughts drift. The aroma of apple blossoms slowly drifted a gentle breeze, the sun was high, as bird songs sauntered by. Fragrant hints of nearby flowers and hay slipped across the air. A discreet red fox magically appeared, sticking his head above the swaying grass. Below the billowing clouds, courageous tiny birds squawked as they pursued an escaping eagle. Ever changing shapes drifted ever so slowly in the clouds. Great mythical beasts appeared floating, then soaring, as if to reach some mystical kingdom high beyond the clouds.

I awoke. How rude of me!
I shall imagine again.

LIGHTING ENCOUNTERS

I have had more than my share of chance meetings with lightning. As a child, gazing out a window, I vividly remember a lightning bolt striking a pine tree, splintering and exploding shards of wood everywhere. Intense light flooded my eyes, as the percussion blast vibrated the rattling window. Stunned, a deafening ringing filled my ears, smoke was billowing up from where the tree had been struck, glowing embers protruded from its wound. Unexplainably, I was not afraid. What lingered in my thoughts was the odd smell. An aroma I cannot explain but would never forget.

As a teenager, my father, brother and I were stream fishing the Great North Woods. A storm came upon us quickly and they hastily scrambled to the car. I, on the other hand, was dragging my feet, because I wanted to get that one last cast. By the time I had reached the top of the mountainous road, I noticed that the hairs on my arms were standing up. For seemingly no reason, I turned to look back from where I had just climbed. A bolt of lightning struck, hitting the tar three feet in front of me, it was encased in some type of auric glow. Feeling movement, my eyes looked down, my feet were off the ground, delivering an overwhelming feeling of floating. Once again, the smell was overpowering and the odor permeated my clothes. Not knowing how, there I was, inside the car. The next thing I remembered was my brother and father laughing and pointing at my hair, which was still standing on end. Laughingly they said, "We have never seen you move so fast in your life!" I was dazed, but kept fishing the rest of the day. The smell persisted that entire day and night. I found out years later that lingering smell was called ozone. Transformed oxygen that leaves behind that particular odor.

These were not to be my last encounters. Twice more while at my father's camp we had close calls. All our hairs were levitating straight up, but no smell, no ringing in the ears and no direct hit from lightning bolts. Incidentally, do not believe that lightning does not strike the same place twice. My house has been hit by lightning four times!

Just a note, when I was playing music in a band, my nickname was "*electric*", even though at that time, I played an acoustic guitar. The band mates had never known about my lighting adventures.

GOLDEN EXPERIENCE

I was visiting my father in Maine for a few days in the early spring. One day, we were gazing out the windows with anticipation for the arrival of the deer, we were not disappointed. The sun was resting just above the trees as two doe came into the yard. Soon after, three more deer showed themselves. There were two yearlings, two doe and one buck. We silently watched as the rays of sun hung on the horizon. My eyes shifted to a movement from across the street. Streaks of light accented a large animal with a golden sheen casually walking from behind the barn of the neighbor's yard. It stopped in the tall swaying grass noticing the deer. Advancing across the road to where I lost sight of what I had thought was a very large dog. Running to another window, I saw it crouching and moving fast through the tall grass behind a large crabapple tree, just out of sight of the deer. Running back to the previous window I noticed the deer had picked up its scent, now thinking it was a coyote. The deer's ears were straight up; their tails were flashing white, as they nervously stomped. I was standing ready to run out and scare the animal away, when it suddenly burst from behind the apple tree and froze. All the deer immediately formed a straight line with the yearlings in the middle, tail's twitching; ears up; all standing tall and alert. It was then the animal turned so that I had a clear look at its entire body. I was struck at its size and color; it was mostly a yellowish gold color, much the same as a golden retriever, but much larger. I do not recall seeing the tail, but most certainly it must have been blonde or gold, or I would have remembered some type of contrast. The deer and the animal stared at each other for quite some time. When the excitement of life explodes before you, time becomes still. The sun fell midway through the trees creating shadows. The courageous deer remained still and tall, stomping their feet. The animal slowly turned and walked down the gravel driveway across the road and into the woods from where it came. The deer's brave behavior had won the day.

Inquiries were made to help me identify the animal; the answers came back swiftly! There had been many sightings in the same town, of what I now know was a golden wolf. This species had evolved from the cross breeding of a coyote and a wolf. A new species of wolf living in Maine.

My first and only encounter, so far, with a golden wolf could not have been more golden.

TWIN FAWNS

One spring afternoon I was relaxing at the desk viewing the back and side fields that lead into three separate wood lines. I was waiting for the deer to arrive as a smiling wind captured my gaze, it gently caressed the fields filling the room with scents of buttercups and clover. Colorful birds hovered and dove in and out, bees briskly flew from flower to flower, as inquisitive racing chipmunks scurried about their chores in life. Serenity flowed through the fields. The deer soon began to cautiously enter from the wood lines. Two twin fawns, that were born in this field, were prancing, and frolicking into a full run trying their best to get the mother to join them. Jumping, sprinting and hopping they surrounded the mother until she finally gave in and joined the fun. Lost in their dance, they cavorted the entire length of the fields. Suddenly, two different fawns pranced their way into the field. Never seeing these two before, I watched the scene play out before me, as the rest of the adults came streaming out. Watching the two new fawns I finally realized that they were bucks. By now, there were at least eight deer and four fawns in the yard. I watched them play and feed as the setting sun fell beneath the trees.

Every evening the deer would faithfully reappear. As time went by, most of the animals had gotten used to my appearance outside and inside the door. They were cautious, yet they would eventually carry on. One day, the buck fawns approached the window, peering in at me seated at the desk. Literally, no more than three feet away. Their heads would tilt from side to side, probably wondering what kind of creature they were staring at. One early evening they peered in, while I had been engrossed in thought. Startled, I had not perceived their approach, a much-needed smile erupted in the reflections of their eyes. Soon after the female fawns began to also trust the window, and the creature behind it. These events became rather routine.

One early summer afternoon I headed out the door into the sun-bathed field, to place three colorful fiberglass rods into the ground. A warm breeze swayed the golden field as butterflies fluttered above. Surveying groundhogs popped their heads up, gossiping to each other as my friend the flycatcher perched above the door watching every movement.

The flycatcher was born with two siblings, under the deck that overlooked my desk. I believe this one was the only one that could actually see me from the nest. When they were learning to fly, I had many happy moments watching them catch insects. My friend however, would bounce off the screens trying to catch them. Ever since then it has followed me around the yard, but I digress.

The setting sun shot colors into the sky as tree shadows began to stretch. I patiently waited for the deer's arrival. Immediately, I noticed the twins did not approach the window. All the deer were noticeably more alert. Thinking over the matter, I theorized that since the fiberglass rods were placed in the ground, the fawns stopped approaching the window. This continued for about a week.

Well, before I could think of the proper solution, one of the curious young bucks decided to test what those things were. Slowly he walked up to the left rod, from my point of view, softly nudging it with his nose. It bent slightly, swinging back towards him just missing its face. Slowly backing up about ten yards the buck intently stared at the middle rod. Fascinated by its behavior a smile burst to my lips; thinking, he really is not contemplating that middle rod. The buck cautiously moved forward, then suddenly reared back, coming down hard on the middle rod. Bending it in half, it came snapping back quickly, hitting him squarely on the nose. He jumped up so high by the time he came down he was at least three deer lengths away from the rods, he promptly fled to the wood line. By this time, I was laughing so hard that all the other deer were staring, moving their heads from left to right, probably wondering what that crazy animal was doing. The fawn had stopped at the wood line and ever so slowly headed back to rejoin the others. It wandered around as if nothing had happened, then finally he stared down the rod on the right. Tears of laughter were streaming down my cheeks, as I sat at the window watching. All the deer were now peering into the window. No way! No way was that deer going for a third try! I was so wrong, it gently walked up and nudged it ever so softly, then walked back with the others. The adventurous buck had received an education, the three poles were not electrified. I shall never underestimate the curiosity, or the intelligence of any animal again.

Both sets of twins have been back to the window, and we have shared many parallel struggles of life.

KNOWING FEAR

It was a cool crisp sunny day as we drove up the hill to visit family. The yard was lightly covered in snow; ancient trees adorned the yard leading to the slate walkway to their door.

Once inside, we were enjoying ourselves when a faint cry for help could be heard. Glancing around we noticed that my son had mysteriously disappeared. Again, we heard the faint cry and realized that it was coming from outside, we all instantly ran out. With sweeping eyes, we scanned the area hoping to find the location of his distress. Another shriek came from the sky. Looking up, searching the trees, he revealed himself. Atop of a twenty-five to-thirty-foot tree, there he was, grasping the tree so tightly that assuredly he was stopping all life from reaching the very top. Everyone tried to talk him down but to no avail. His curiosity and sense of adventure had led him to discover he had a fear of heights. I blurted out flippantly, "Who would like to go up and get him?" Immediately, my sister's son, a youngster with wisdom beyond his years, shouted "It must be you; you are his father!" Somewhat embarrassed, I realized he spoke the truth. I do not remember how I traversed the first six feet to the first branch, yet I am quite sure that someone assisted me, or some tool aided my ascent. It was then, for the very first time, I experienced fear. My son had a fearless behavior, yet I was not sure he had the understanding that adventures must be carefully thought through. Fear struck deep within me, realizing it was up to me to save both of us. With each step, watching his eyes, while I spoke softly to him. Thinking to myself; would the branches hold my weight? Climbing nearer to him, wondering if he would panic as I got closer and try to jump to me. Would the smaller branches break from the extra weight? I could see and feel his fear when I finally touched his leg. He instantly became calm with no sign of panic. Relieved, I said, "look at me, look into my eyes, I will not let you fall. I will hold and place your foot on each branch as you step down until the branches can hold both of us." I was feeling the fear rush through my body, as we descended. We both endured as he held me tightly navigating the rest of the way down. Surely, all were relieved when he was handed down to waiting arms. Then we all enjoyed the precious time we had together.

For some time, my son and I spoke of how we could share new adventures that would stimulate the adrenaline. Finally, we decided to give parachuting a try. Relax! Not the kind you jump out of a plane, the kind you dress in a squirrel suit, and float high inside a building. It was truly exhilarating! We have enjoyed quite a few free floats and hope to keep enjoying them. As a team, minds and courage conquer.

THE LOST STAR
Ken & Aaron Skoby

It had been a long hard day at work as my son and I pulled into the driveway and walked to the porch that overlooked the backyard. The clear warm summer night beckoned to us as we paused and stared above the hardwood treeline into the glittering sky. Our hope was to witness a few falling meteors or shooting stars which we had seen many times before. The night was still, the air was saturated with the fragrances from the various flower gardens. Captivated, but exhausted, we decided to take a midnight swim in the pool. A quick run, jump and dive, we were submersed in the soothing water. The twinkling stars beckoned our eyes as we surveyed the heavens quietly. All the heat and stress of the long day was disappearing. We became suspended in silence.

I was staring into the sky above the treeline, but this night my son was looking into the sky above the house. To my left and his right was a long pathway adorned with arches of bowing white birches guiding one into an evergreen forest. We seldom watched this part of the sky because the house blocked that particular view from the porch. As we drifted in silence, time became insignificant.

While gazing thoughtfully into the sky, my eyes were drawn to the left where a pulsating light appeared. The scintillating star burst forth with arms of light reaching through space in the silence. The star gradually got larger and brighter, almost blinding. Mesmerized, I watched it expand and explode, lighting up the atmosphere. Then it blinked and the brilliant light disappeared and faded into nothingness. We both pondered in silence for quite some time. Synchronized, we both spoke in harmony. 'Did you see that? What was that?" We had both realized that we had seen something very special. I had theorized that we had just seen the death of a star, yet we were not sure.

My Son Aaron's Perspective

Can death create life? How could the end of one thing be the creation of something entirely new? With every passing, a memory is made that will live on forever. Take the simple passing of time. In the infinite second between one click of the second hand on a clock to the next, billions of moments happen all around the world. A child's first core memory. A dog rescued by its forever family. A tree catches fire in a storm and destroys an entire forest.

For better or worse, life comes, life goes. But it forever goes on. Until it doesn't.

One unassuming Saturday night you may look up into the endless void of space while your down in your backyard, swimming in your pool with your father after a long day of work. This night, you may both be looking at the same star, at the same time, for no other reason than your eyes just gazed to this one glimmer of light coincidently. One night, you may see something that at the time is unexplainable. The star begins to brighten, growing and expanding, then exploding in the sky as if the curtain of the veil to our cosmos was being bombarded by the explosion. Silent. Sudden. Bright.

Then nothing.

In the infinite second between expansion and illumination, to the second tick of the clock; a sudden and aggressive silence, your body and mind work in beautiful symmetry, stone still and awestruck.

What did I see? Did I actually see it? Was I so tired from the days labors that my mind played a trick on me? Surely my father would have spoken up, seeing how strange it was. I must have been mistaken. Then I looked at him at the exact moment he looked at me. The look in his eyes said it all. We both saw the unexplainable. We both shared something strange, wonderful, sad and unique. We both had the same shared flashes. We could only share the silence of the moment, as the sounds of crickets and gentle leaves in the winds finally began to return us to our senses.

After many years you may find out that this event was in fact the death of a star. This may surprise you, or sadden you. Make you wonder if you will ever see something like it again.

It doesn't matter because even with the death of something; that which has witnessed countless lifetimes beyond measure and kept its own corner of the cosmos lit with a unique glow, has given birth to a memory of two people which will last forever in their hearts.

Life comes from death. Death creates a memory which lives in us for better or worse. It brings a father and son closer together with a memory that is special just to them, which they will always share together no matter the direction, distance or differences in their lives. Their shared recollection is a lifelong memory they will always cherish. The irony will never be lost and the gratitude for the final act of a star, light years away, helped a son connect with his father. That will stay forever within me.

SEEDS

It was a brisk colorful fall morning; vagrant winds caressed the flowers and fields as the last of the fragrant aromas of life began to fade. Flowers slowly waved to the last of their days, withering and drying. Nomadic critical winds spread their seeds across the land. Many of the seeds landed softly in groups in the spacious fields, others rested about the cool shaded wood line in smaller groups, but one seed fell into a crevasse of a rock that overlooked the field and woodland. The icy fingers of winter soon arrived, dormant seeds slumbered under a sentimental white blanket, dreaming of what their new life would bring.

As the spring rains arrived, some seeds were lost to various vibrantly feathered birds, while others slowly began to awaken and sprout. The flowing fields and woodlands began turning emerald green, as all life peered about discovering their new surroundings. As they grew, they swayed in the gentling winds and soaked in the wisdom of a nurturing sun. The flowers went about their days growing and swaying to the vibrations of the winds, rains, and sun. The undetected seed upon the rock had not yet released, but as time went by, the seed began to sprout. The unyielding sprout relaxed, bathing in raindrops and reaching up to the soothing light of an ancient sun and moon. Warm dancing summer winds caressed all, as they sprouted and grew. Birds soared, various majestic trees bowed, and soft mystical silhouetted clouds floated the vast blue skies. After the rains the single seed watched vibrant rainbows appear in the distance, it felt thunder and lightning, sunrises, and sunsets. Witnessing babbling brooks and tranquil ponds, magnificent lakes and great mountains with rushing rivers cascading down to touch the sea. It observed great beasts walking by. The climbing flower waltzed in melodic winds as it embraced all that reached it. As the sun bathed the rock, the flower became aware that those that once towered above, were now dwarfed below. Noticing that some of their stalks had bends and breaks while it's stalk was long and straight. Some of the flowers had struggled and wilted, as they moved closer to the warmth of the autumn rock. Others had passed, yet there on the rock the sun caressed that single flower for many more weeks. All had lived every moment, and released their seeds to the winds.

THE ODD DUCKS

Curiously, a male duck walked to shore. Slowly other ducks of the same species landed and followed. First three ducks, then five ducks, then seven ducks, all followed each other around realizing they were comfortable together. The males were quite beautiful, with a yellow bill, shiny green heads, with a white ring around their lower neck. They had a chocolate brown breast, with a centered black tail that curled up as if they had just come from the feather salon. The females had an orange bill with a stripe of black, their bodies were predominantly shadings of brown with black accents. Both sexes share white tails and white beneath their wings, and in the center of the outer wings a brilliant blue, accented at each end in white. They all happily existed together watching over their young, as they swam and ate. Feeling safe and warm, they slept.

Suddenly, one day flying in unannounced from their long flight, three ducks landed onto the lake to feed and rest. There was an intense silence. Who were these ducks? They did not look like the other ducks; they surely did not belong. Their feathers were not the same colors, their bodies were smaller and their wings had different markings. Despite trying to introduce his mate and duckling, the resting ducks did not like these new ducks landing so close to them. So, they chased them away onto the bank.

A silent kingfisher regally landed on a branch overlooking the scene, quietly watching. The family bathed in the sun. Suddenly the father duck noticed something large in the sky and quickly swam to tell the others of the danger. He was promptly chased away again. The family watched in horror as a great eagle swooped down into the group, carrying one of the ducklings away. Turmoil and quacking filled the air. The lake's disrupted waters rippled and waved, finally becoming still. Feathers floated upon the surface of the lake; as a compassionate wind blew the feathers across the calm waters. They all sat solemnly, yet still rejected the new family. The brave father duck waddled up to the kingfisher and conversed with the regal bird. The kingfisher flew from its perch to converse with a cardinal. The cardinal flew off to converse with the friendly chickadees. The chickadees spoke to many others.

The next day the kingfisher returned, landing on his throne surveying. The same scene began to unfold. The family kept its distance, then came to the shore to rest. The cardinal flew by and landed on the branch next to the kingfisher. The chickadees sounded the alarm, as the kingfisher flew up and dove into the middle of the large gathering of ducks causing them to scatter. The chickadees swiftly flew up into the face of danger, chirping wildly. to where the eagle flew. They courageously chased the frightened eagle across the sky. The cardinal nodded and sang, because he knew, they all had finally realized they were not all the same, yet they faced the same dangers, together even the smallest showed courage.

United, all flew together, yet
each took separate paths to different journeys.

*Wisdom may be discovered
at anytime, anywhere and from all life*

THE MOLA AND THE SPARROW

An early morning haze hung above the bay as the sun shone down on the two fishermen as they loaded their gear into the sixteen foot boat. They rushed around wildly making sure they had not missed anything that they might need. Launching the boat, an immediate sense of calm swept over them as they slowly motored through the low hanging fog of the sea. Anticipation filled their thoughts as they headed off to Jeffery's Ledge, twenty six miles away. The welcoming sun quickly burned the mysterious mist away as they arrived at their first stop. Immediately, they started catching haddock. When the pace slowed they would move and try another spot. As the day slipped away they decided to head back to the bay to try one more spot.

While fishing, they noticed an ocean sunfish basking in the sun about thirty yards away. Having enough haddock, they decided to take a closer look at the unique fish. They slowly motored over then drifted towards the magnificent six foot mola. Much to their surprise, the fish headed straight towards the boat and began circling it. The fishermans first thoughts were it looked as if some great beast had slipped up behind it and taken an enormous bite out of its body.

Mesmerized, they watched in silence as it circled. It's eye seemed to look straight into their souls, as it moved ever so slowly by. Entering the sea with a hand, the fish slowly swam by allowing one of them to stroke its seemingly soft skin. Remaining silent, they bathed in the joy of its encounter. Excited smiling faces erupted, as they spoke of each other's personal experiences with the fish, as they slowly headed back towards the bay, still about twenty miles away.

As they talked, a song sparrow flew in and landed on the tip of one of the fishing poles. The poor distressed bird was panting trying to catch its breath, as it just sat there, exhausted. We wondered. How did this bird trust and know to land here? What would have happened if we had not stopped to experience the mola? How did this bird end up way out here? One of the fishermen thought of a plausible solution. He supposed that the bird had been on a large barge and was taken far out to sea. They both agreed that was the solution for the bird's journey.

By this time, the bird had become more relaxed as it quietly listened to the playful banter of the fishermen. Bobbing its head back and forth, it suddenly spoke, chirping away joining in the conversation. The three continued their chatter as a faint land mass appeared on the shadowed horizon. Every now and then the bird chirped and sang. Soon the boat came upon the shoals, the three knew they were nearing the end of another one of life's wonderous adventures. They all watched as spirited seals swam in and out of the waves peering in the direction of the boat with their dark playful eyes. The colorful sky caught a setting sun as they passed the shoals. The song sparrow nodded and flew off in the direction of the bay. No last chirp, no fly by, it headed straight for home, as were the fishermen. Entering the harbor, tying up to the dock they slowly found their land legs. Smiling, they paused for one last gaze over the bay, as the sun reflected upon the shimmering waters that had left jewels in their souls.

    Nature is extremely profound.

THE CONCERT

I was awakened very early one morning by a melodic three noted bird song just outside my opened window. Lying in bed hearing it again, I quickly rushed to search into the darkness for its source. Peering out into the charcoal darkness of the sky, my wandering eyes could not find the bird. Who was this mysterious songster? Heading back to bed, I once again heard its notes, hastily I crept to the opened window. The rain from the night before had washed the pollen from the trees and sky, as I deeply inhaled the fragrant pure air. With a sweeping glance I still could not locate the mysterious songster. Something just did not feel right, birds normally do not sing this early. I quickly got dressed and headed outside into the damp field, searching for a suitable spot to listen for the source of the song. The air was quiet as I peered into the wood, still searching for the mysterious musician. A down draft of shifting air alerted my senses to a low flying raven just above. From inside the wood line a few birds started chirping. Mystified, a strange sensation engulfed the area.

There is a time between the dark and dawn and sunset and blackness when a quiet peace surrounds the atmosphere. Yet, birds inside the wood line were speaking to each other, some from a great distance away. I could tell there were four or five different species conversing, some more boisterous than others. It was if they were at a town hall meeting debating points of view over some impending crisis that had to be addressed. Was there a new predator in the woods? Back and forth it went for quite some time, as the darkened sky began its transformation to grays. The crescendo started as the birds began to interrupt and talk over each other. Suddenly there was an intense silence. A raven flew back over the trees. The sun began to peek, throwing colors through the clouds, the grays were transforming into blues. A single bird sang, then another and another, together floating a symphony across the woods and field. All the birds' tones harmonized with each other, as melodies soared through the sky; the silky vibrations engulfed me in wonder. Their soft voices soared into a transcendent climax.

An empty hush cloaked the air as a mystical breeze slowly caressed the calm. A single duck flew high above, two airborne sparrows swooped low taking their bow and flew into the trees. Entertained, I joyfully greeted the newly born day. I never did discover the mysterious songster.

The next morning while sitting at my desk, which views the bird feeders, two chickadees landed on the screen of my opened window, seemingly quite disturbed. They peered into the room, not three feet from me, staring into my eyes, chirping wildly. One of the birds' feathers were ruffled, as they clung to the screen squawking to me. After a short pause, I asked them what their problem was as I glanced again at the bird feeders to see if they were filled. I had to smile wondering what had caused them to raise such a ruckus. The distressed chirping started up again and lasted for quite some time, then they just flew away. The encounter made me grin the rest of the day.

The next morning, to my surprise, the scene unfolded once again. This time with a pair of goldfinches. I immediately knew I was missing something. So, after they had their say, I went outside to the bird feeders and looked around for feathers or anything out of the ordinary. Twice more I checked the feeders, still, finding no clues. By now I was sure these birds were trying to convey something.

On the third morning I woke early and waited at my desk to see what would happen. I was not surprised by the appearance of two song sparrows repeating the scenes of the last two days. Grasping the screen and skreiching in distress. I was now beside myself; I did not understand what they all were trying to convey, but I knew something must be seriously wrong. That was to be the last visit to my window screen.

I was puzzled and must admit I had no idea what was wrong. I searched again, this time wandering into to the wood line to where I had heard them singing four days earlier. I saw nothing out of the ordinary, but again, I was not sure what I was looking for.

The next few days I was very vigilant and noticed that the hummingbirds had become very possessive at their two feeders chasing each other away, even though the feeders were about six feet apart. The number of birds at the three seed feeders seemed to be diminishing. The goldfinches seemingly just disappeared. Finally, I noticed a group of about thirty starlings taking over the area. I would go out about three or more times a day to chase them away. I knew that once the farms in the area had planted their crops that the birds would eventually move away. So, that lasted for about six weeks. That problem did go away, but it took almost two months for all the birds to return. I have no idea if the starlings were the root of the problem, however, I do know that the birds were trying to tell me something.

CLOSE ENCOUNTERS

Launching the boat, the three friends headed out into the great unknown, not knowing that this day was not to be just another at sea. Bearing off to the southeast, basking in the vibrant rising sun, two talked about a past adventure that the other had missed.

It was a morning like this as we stopped to catch some bait fish near one of our favorite locations, just in case we ran into tuna or strippers. The ocean was still, the view was peaceful as we watched a few lobster fishermen haul in their pots. Gulls and terns declared their intentions while floating in the air above. We began to catch a number of bait fish. Within the hour we found ourselves surrounded by boats, one being a large charter boat. Having caught enough bait, we headed into the open ocean, arriving at our first stop. We dropped our lines and started to fish. In the distance, we could hear whales blowing out water to take in air. The ocean was calm, the sky was clear as a wandering breeze cooled us. We started to catch a few haddock immediately. Once again, we noticed boats seemed to be surrounding us. So, we decided to reel up our lines and head for another area. Arriving at our next destination, we drifted and dropped our lines and began to question what the heck was going on. Seemly, we were being followed everywhere we went. This time, boats much larger than ours showed up and parked in parallel lines to the left and right of us, dropping their anchors, with us in the middle, at the end. Three to the left of us, two to the right. Then a very large whale watching charter dropped anchor to our right. We looked at each other quite puzzled saying "they know something we do not." We decided to stay even though we felt crowded, mostly because we were tired of moving. No one likes to keep reeling up line from two hundred feet, unless there is a fish on it. We then noticed that people on the charter boat were pointing and laughing and many of them began to take pictures of us. Probably wondering, what were those two crazy guys in a sixteen-foot boat, seventeen if you count the motor, doing more than twenty miles out at sea. We calmly, ignored the commotion as we sat and fished with our backs to the boats. This time not catching fish! The peaceful silence was shattered when a number of people yelled, whale! We snapped our heads around to watch a very large whale descending, heading straight for our boat. To put it mildly, uncertainty set in when we saw a mother and a baby whale surfacing to breathe, right between the line of boats.

They were headed straight for us! Our eyes popped wide open as an eerie silence surrounded the air. We furiously began to reel up our lines, thinking the whales might get caught up in them. Once the lines were in, at a record rate I might add; we dropped our poles and grasped a rail of the boat while gazing into the water. Hearts were pounding as we prepared for a collision. Relief arrived when we saw nothing after what I thought was a few seconds. Laughing we put the motor in gear and off we went again. As we drove away the ribbing started. "You should have seen your face!" "Yeah, well I noticed your white knuckles in a death grip on the rail." Reinvigorated, relief laughter filled the air, as we stopped at our next destination. While drifting, a very large whale's tail erupted no more than ten yards away, pulling the boat right over to the smooth waters of its descent. Lastly, yet just as exciting, we got to witness a total breach of a very large whale, from a much safer distance. One cannot help but think that whales are highly intelligent with just a bit of flair. When we pulled into the dock that afternoon, as luck would have it, tying up right behind that whale watching boat. We were greeted with smiles and waves. "Hey you are the guys in that small boat." The stories continued as the three friends reached their destination, dropping their lines at one of their favorite destinations.

Laughter echoed in the waves, as we all caught a few fish. Meanwhile, the time seemingly drifted away. A change in the tide and winds delivered swift currents and three-foot waves. So, we all decided that it was probably a good idea to head for shore. We slowly headed back towards land. The usual jokes started immediately. Who caught the biggest, who caught the most keepers, who was the oldest? The usual friendship banter kept up as the waves broke over the boat. Somewhere between here and there, a voice shouted. "Look, look; what are those things?" Whatever they were, they were immense! Silence hung in the air, not a word was spoken, as we saw another and another. We each had our own moments, realizing every second would be priceless. I could only see shadows of gigantic beasts of unbelievable size, because I was not wearing my polarized sunglasses, but that was enough. They were very reminiscent of submarines. I quickly remedied my situation and put on my polarized sunglasses. The sounds of wind and waves echoed as we struggled to make sense of what we were seeing. "What are those things?" "I think they are basking sharks." As we were discussing the experiences, an even larger one appeared with another following it a bit behind. It was as if they had heard our voices. Forgotten vigor and excitement surrounded the boat. We all were quite sure that this was a once in a lifetime event. We quietly stared into the waters watching them slowly fade in and out of sight. By now the shoals were just coming into view, any tensions about the waves and tide had slipped away. We were about to have an experience far beyond what we had just witnessed.

A bellowing voice broke the quiet of our serene thoughts. "Two more, heading straight for us! Put the motor in neutral!" Drifting slowly, we observed two basking sharks heading straight for the boat. A smaller one and one more massive than any of the others previously observed. The goliath leisurely swam up to the back of the boat, where all three bodies were cramped together for a better view. The giant basking shark gradually swam forward, to about a foot away from the back of the motor, there it suspended. Its head was enormous! As I looked into one of its eyes, it stared back into the three sets of astonished eyes. It was at this point, as if hypnotized, I became engulfed in a gentle calmness, time and space seemed to disappear. It was as if I was sharing some type of ancient wisdom from this being. My thoughts wandered in a magnificent glow as it hovered, barely moving. We were floating in the sea of time, when the intense quite was shattered, when someone shouted. "Maybe its hungry, give it a fish." A fish dropped, bouncing off its head; it turned and followed it into the deep. It slowly came back from underneath the boat, then circled and suspended to the back again. This was when the three realized the shark was well over thirty feet in length. It lingered, and was promptly given another fish which was quickly swallowed. We all stood not three feet away as it opened its enormous mouth. In that moment, I noticed for the first time, its mouth extended far beyond both sides of the back of the boat. An immediate sense of insignificance and humility slipped into my mind. Its beauty and grace shone brightly on its black reflective body, as it floated in stillness in the rippling water. My mind struggled to comprehend the size of its opened mouth, yet no fear ever entered. Still to this day, I cannot comprehend the profound significance of this chance encounter that we shared. Eventually, the basking shark slowly backed away. The motor was once again put in gear as we slowly pulled away heading in the direction of the bay. I slowly, not gracefully, walked back to the front of the boat and sat down. My thoughts scattered as we motored on. Was it curious, hungry or was it just trying to guide us back to the shore?

The motor was once again put in neutral so we could check our bearings to be sure we were headed in the correct direction. Thoughts dissolved when my friend yelled from the back of the boat. "It's coming back! It's getting close! Gun it!" The motor wailed, jerking us backwards and back into reality. My thoughts drifted. Did it think we were stranded? Was it going to help us get back to shore? I supposed it really did not matter, I was grateful for the time and experience they shared with us.

The large basking shark disappeared from view for a short time, then met up with the smaller one, reappearing, and following us from a safe distance. The seas got a little rougher as we approached the shoals. Our new friends followed us for about three more miles. Veering off to the south, our two new friends slipped from our sight. We could now see our destination. Silence hung in the air for the next few miles, speaking volumes of our experience. The significance of this day surely will be with us for a lifetime.

Silently, we slipped into the bay.

THE AWAKENING

It was a starry night as the young man gazed up into the heavens, hoping to catch glimmers of shooting stars crossing the sky. The nearing full moon smiled down, accepting his nightly flight from the world below. On rainy nights he would walk the streets just to feel gentle droplets touch his face. Slowly descending to the mazes below, sounds assaulted his ears, his eyes were flooded by flashing hypnotic artificial lights. As he wandered through the jungle of steel, tar, and stones, he sensed ghosts floating the dusty polluted streets.

One night on the way to his retreat, he noticed something odd. Walking toward the scene, he came upon a man in tattered clothes lying unconscious. Approaching closer, kneeling, he noticed blood was flowing from his forehead. The young man took off his shirt and placed it under the injured man's head. The smell of alcohol rose from his seemingly lifeless body. Hollow humans, some dressed in the finest clothes, passed by, glancing down in disgust at the shirtless young man and his tattered companion. His sweeping eyes searched for help. Noticing a long window that met the sidewalk, emitting lights, he peered in. Not noticing anyone, he decided to get to a telephone and call for help.

Upon his return, the young man noticed people, still walking by, some laughing and pointing, some even kicking the limp body. Heartbroken, he waited for the ambulance to arrive. Upon their arrival and departure, he stood alone, dazed. Kneeling to pick up his bloody shirt, he noticed a smiling elderly gentleman behind the glass, beckoning him to come in. Wandering to the steps that led down into the shop, the smiling man was already standing there with the door opened. Confused and dazed, the young man entered the shop. The elderly man moved slowly, his weathered body, reaching for a pot of hot tea as his trembling hands poured it into a small cup. He promptly gave it to the young man to drink. His aged fingers gently touched the young man's shoulder, as the gentle smile left his face. He bowed. It was as if he had watched and felt what the young man had just been through. He was a seemingly kind man; his body held an aura of wisdom and serenity. The smile reappeared as he pointed to items in his shop, signaling for the young man to come and see. The shop was small, yet every space, shelf and draw were filled with wonders. The young man was not familiar with what he was looking at, or what the elderly man was saying. Somehow, they both understood each other. On the shelves were apothecary jars filled with colorful powders, and herbs, boxes of exotic teas and foods. Mysterious aromas softly drifted through the air. Drawers were filled with leaves, roots and flowers from a variety of plants. Others were filled with dried insects, bones, hairs, teeth and claws from various animals. The young man signaled that he must be going and headed for the door. At the door they paused, touched their hearts, and bowed.

The next day, wanting to thank the elderly man, the young man headed back to the shop. Upon entering he was greeted with an immediate excited smile. The young man's gestures spoke. Pointing to himself, shaking his head back and forth, clenching his fist, pounding his heart, raising his arms and flexing. The elderly man momentarily pondered, then reached for a box from one of the shelves, placing his solution on the counter. The young man paid and bowed as he left the shop.

One day the young man stopped by to see his friend as he was closing and locking his shop. Traversing the stairs from the shop to the sidewalk, he smiled, gesturing for the young man to follow. They both walked about four steps when the aged man turned, opening a door, gesturing to come in. The young man stared up at a long dimly lit stairway that disappeared into darkness. Feeling forlorn for his friend, assuming he was traversing the rail less stairs every day to reach home. The young man walked behind his friend in the event that he might stumble. Each stair had its story, as the ancient wood creaked and bent with the weight of every step. Ascending the stairs, the astonished young man gazed into an enormous hall. Seven twenty-foot tables filled with people sitting quietly, half the group sat with their backs to the stairs. Soon they had all turned gazing in the direction for the two men. Placing his hand on his friends' shoulder, the elderly man spoke, his arm moving wildly about, as smiles were starting to erupt everywhere. All the shining eyes turned to the young man and bowed in his direction. The young man bowed in return, having no idea what was said or why they were smiling or bowing. The group then returned to their serenity, quietly eating. The two friends advanced to a barred window, with a large opening at the bottom. The elderly man pointed above, to a list of characters, apparently listing choices of foods. Puzzled, shrugging his shoulders, wide eyes gazing for assistance from his friend. The elderly man smiled and thoughtfully ordered two meals, which the younger man quickly paid for. Consenting people swiftly shifted about to accommodate the two friends, they all sat in silence eating. Finishing their meals, they traversed down the stairs entering the street, each bowing, and leaving in separate directions.

The young man pondered the wonder filled evening. Overwhelmed by the joys of finding a new friend, picturing the smiling faces and shining eyes of strangers, and the gift of savory foods. A rogue tear escaped his eye and fell upon cheerful lips. He walked silently smiling through the bleak dark jungle to his room.

Many times, in the following months, the two shared gestures, and smiles in the elderly man's shop. Sharing life, they dined together at the same place many more times, to the point where one day the young man traversed the talking stairs alone…

 Realizing in even the dense darkest hour,
  a light will shine unexpectedly,
   when needed the most.

THE TOUCH

Our body is a machine
Let the soul be its guide

We search and search
for the meaning of life
while the entire time
it is surrounding us

The greatest moments are in front of us
We must move forward to receive them

Time is our most valuable gift
share it with others

Love cannot be possessed
it must be held gently

THANK YOU

www.ingramcontent.com/pod-product-compliance
Lightning Source LLC
LaVergne TN
LVHW061035070526
838201LV00073B/5047